A Guide to Locating

ROCKY MOUNTAIN WILDFLOWERS

Parry's Primrose — PRIMULA PARRYI

by **Panayoti Kelaidis**

A RENAISSANCE HOUSE PUBLICATION

© Copyright 1994 by Panayoti Kelaidis. Printed in the United States of America. All rights reserved. This book or any parts thereof, may not be reproduced in any manner whatsoever without written permission of the publisher:

ISBN: 1-55838-148-1

RENAISSANCE HOUSE
A Division of Jende-Hagan, Inc.
541 Oak Street ~ P.O. Box 177
Frederick, CO 80530

Cover photo and all interior photos courtesy Robert Heapes

10 9 8 7 6 5 4 3 2 1

WELCOME

Thousands of kinds of wildflowers occur in the Rocky Mountain region. More than 100 varieties of penstemons grow here, even more types of daisies, and almost as many kinds of buckwheats. This area has such extraordinary biodiversity that it is impossible to illustrate all the regional plants in one small volume. The flowers in this book were selected because they are the plants travelers are most likely to see on drives and walks through the Rockies.

If the exact species you're looking at isn't in this book, you're likely to find a close relative with similar habits and associations. When in doubt on identification, remember that the general traits of leaf and stem can vary tremendously in wet or dry years. Flower color is a subjective and variable characteristic. Look closely at the shape of the blossom, count the petals, and note details on the interior of the plant's blossom. These criteria will help make your identification more certain.

When wildflower hunting, try to stay on paths and roads. Enjoy the plants, but leave them as you find them. If you are inspired to grow native plants in your garden, seek guidance in books or at Rocky Mountain nurseries, most of which stock a wide variety of native wildflowers in pots or as seed. Not only do wild plants rarely make good garden specimens, digging or even picking wildflowers is illegal and strictly prosecuted in many western states!

Photographs in this book were taken by Robert E. Heapes, wildflower and wildlife photographer. His work appears in many books and national publications. Bob has a special interest in botanical history, and is authoring a book about the early army exploration of the Rocky Mountain region.

The author, Panayoti Kelaidis, lectures on alpines world-wide. He has pioneered the cultivation of the cold deserts of the American West, many of which were once thought to be difficult or impossible to cultivate. He has cultivated over 5000 species of high mountain plants in recent decades, many of which are on public display at Denver Botanic Gardens' Rock Alpine Garden where he is employed as curator.

PANAYOTI KELAIDIS

ROBERT HEAPES

Contents

Welcome 2
Narcissus Flowered Anemone 4
Colorado Columbine 5
Prickly Poppy 6
Mariposa Lily 7
Marsh Marigold / Globeflower 8
Fairyslipper 9
Plains Paintbrush / Subalpine Paintbrush 10
Rabbitbrush 11
Alpine Spring Beauty 12
Western Clematis 13
Purple Ball Cactus 14
Yellow Ladyslipper 15
Nelson's Larkspur 16
Shooting Star .17
Orange Sneezeweed 18
Claret Cup Cactus 19
Alpine Buckwheat 20
Glacier Lily 21
Parry's Gentian 22
Fremont's Geranium 23
Alumroot 26
Old Man Of The Mountain / Perky Sue 27
Fairy Trumpets 28
Bitter Root 29
Wood Lily 30
Twinflower 31
Blue Flax 32
Creeping Hollyberry 33
Languid Ladies 34
Yellow Monkey Flower / Purple Monkey Flower.35
Nuttall's Evening Primrose 36
Little Red Elephant 37
Penstemons / Alpine Cushion Phlox 38
Sky Pilot 40
Primroses 41
Pasqueflower .42
Moss Campion 43
Cowboy's Delight 44
Golden Banner 45
Alpine Clover .46
Nuttall's Violet .47
Mule's Ears 48

ANEMONE NARCISSIFLORA SSP. ZEPHYRA

Narcissus Flowered Anemone

Most of the anemones that grow in the Rockies have relatively small flowers in muted yellows, reds or dishwater white, and most produce woolly balls of seed in the summer. The narcissus flowered anemone grows among willows or on grassy tundra right around tree line in the southern Rockies. Its much larger cousins reappear in Alaska and occur abundantly throughout the high mountains of Eurasia, from the Alps to the Pyrenees.

The Rocky Mountain subspecies of this anemone looks like a jonquil from a distance--but with a rich boss of yellow anthers instead of a yellow cup in the center of the flower. As the flower ages, these anthers transform into a ball of dark, scale-like seed utterly unlike any other local anemone. There are usually three, occasionally more flowers on the foot-tall flowering stem, which clearly distinguishes it from marsh marigolds and globeflowers that often grow nearby. The leaves are produced in a mound of basal foliage, dark green and less succulent than the deeply incised leaves of globeflowers.

This anemone is particularly abundant in the Mosquito Range and Saguache Mountains of central Colorado, but also grows thickly in spots along Trail Ridge Road in Rocky Mtn. N.P. Look for it to bloom in late June and early July.

AQUILEGIA CAERULEA

COLORADO COLUMBINE

The Rocky Mountain region is a major center of diversity for columbines: no fewer than a dozen different kinds exist here. In moist, shady conifer woods on the western slopes of the Rockies, two scarlet and yellow columbines occur with nodding flowers. In the northern Rockies this is *Aguilegia formosa*, growing a yard or more tall. The much smaller *A. elegantula* is common in New Mexico, Utah and Colorado, with streamlined long-spurred flowers that are a favorite of hummingbirds. Warmer canyons throughout the southern Rockies may have scattered bright yellow columbines with brash up-facing flowers.

The alpine aristocrat is unquestionably Jones' alpine columbine that forms huddled mounds of icy blue foliage and almost stemless, upfacing pure blue flowers. This always grows on shifting, limestone rubble, sometimes by the thousands, at the highest elevations, from central Wyoming to Alberta.

In the month after the summer solstice, aspen woods and alpine meadows often fill with the spectacular Colorado Columbine. The span of this flower's 5 outer segments can exceed 4". These are usually a deep lavender-blue in the southern Rockies, while in Utah and in the northern Rockies the entire flower is often a ghostly white. The plant can stand 36" in lush meadows and woodland, but in drier pastures and above tree line, compact races have evolved that are less than a foot high.

ARGEMONE POLYANTHEMOS

PRICKLY POPPY

Farmers in the Rockies think of these as weeds, in contrast to an English visitor's description of the "dazzling poppywort". The plant's name comes from thick, blue-gray leaves with wavy margins that end in painful prickles. But the flowers, its principal glory, are pure white with a satiny texture, 4" or more wide.

These rather stocky, yard-high plants occur on roadsides and dry meadows, usually in sandy or gravelly soils, from the Great Plains to the upper foothills in the middle and southern Rockies. A constant succession of flowers is produced from late May through the summer in cooler years; but out of bloom, travelers might mistake prickly poppy for a thistle.

Two local native alpine poppies occur on the highest tundra and measure only a few inches tall. One is a pale lemonade yellow, found in the southern Rockies; the bright reddish-orange occur farther north. The giant orange and scarlet cups of Oriental poppies have naturalized in a number of places near town sites. The bright red corn poppies will persist for many years where wildflower seeds have been loosed from a can.

Herbalists have used parts of this plant to treat warts, skin ulcerations, corneal opacities, heat rash, hives, jock rot, urethra and prostate inflamations, sunburn, abrasions, and sleep disorders. But beware: the juice is not only mildly narcotic, but also cathartic.

CALOCHORTUS GUNNISONII

MARIPOSA LILY

Mariposas are immediately distinguishable from other lilies of the Rockies by their huge flowers which measure 3" or more across. These flowers consist of exactly 3 petals, each with fantastic eye spots at the base of the cup-like flower. The shape and nature of these markings is the principal method botanists use to determine individual species of mariposa. In California, dozens of species occur in numerous colors, but travelers in the Rockies usually find only a handful of species and color phases.

The sego lily--state flower of Utah--occurs at lower altitudes, usually on clay soils that are quite alkaline. Sego lilies are a glowing cream color with glistening mahogany-colored oval eye spots at the base of the cup. Yellow forms in Utah's southern Canyonlands have been segregated as a separate species (*C. aureus*); and deep pink varieties are frequent in parts of the San Rafael Swell and the Uinta Basin.

Gunnison's mariposa lily usually grows at higher altitudes, on richer, moister loams of the southern Rocky Mountains. It has crescent-shaped eye spots and cool, white flowers that occasionally come in lavender or purple. In one small part of New Mexico they can be yellow as well. They bloom in shortgrass prairie in mid-June, among open pinewoods and aspen through July, and even above tree line into August.

CALTHA LEPTOSEPALA

Marsh Marigold & Globeflower

Travelers to the Rocky Mountains in June can be nearly certain of finding wet meadows filled with marsh marigold. These are easily distinguished from globeflowers or anemones, among which they often grow, by the oval leaves with scalloped margins. The leaves form a neat foliage ruffle around the flowering stems, which are usually less than a foot high. The flowers--milky white on top but blue as whey on their undersurfaces--have 8 or more segments. Marsh marigolds occur in astonishing abundance wherever soils stay moist late in the season. In the mountains, this is usually well above 9000 ft.

Globeflowers, marsh marigolds' most common companions in nature, have lush, green, divided leaves cut into narrow lobes in a birdfoot pattern. Fortunate travelers may encounter vast drifts of globeflower in the low alpine zone or growing along streams in the dark spruce-fir forests that constitute dominant tree growth below timberline. Its flowers have only 5 segments and are a translucent, lemonade color.

These two harbingers of subalpine spring are an exquisite sight, growing in a random pattern of vivid white and moonlight yellow. Together they produce luminous ribbons of color along streamsides during the weeks when snow melts quickly in the high country.

CALYPSO BULBOSA

FAIRYSLIPPER

While the yellow ladyslipper is a very local and rather rare plant, there are still places in the Rockies where fairyslippers occur by the hundreds or even thousands. Only the most extravagant fairy would wear such a sculpturesque and roccoco slipper--speckled and splashed with deep rose pink. The flower is about 2" long, but because it is one of the first to bloom in the dark, subalpine woodland, it seems positively dramatic. It occurs frequently on the fringes of dense Engelmann spruce/alpine fir woods, from 8000 ft. in the northern Rockies to 12,000 ft. in the southern Rockies.

The entire plant goes dormant with the first hot days of summer, and it takes an experienced eye to notice that the single, heart-shaped seersucker leaf reappears in early autumn. There is evidence that calypsos are mildly saprophytic and derive some of their sustenance from a symbiotic relationship with a fungus that feeds on rotting forest duff.

As with other native orchids, they have never been grown successfully (or predictably) from seed, and collecting them for cultivation is tantamount to murder. Fairyslippers require extremely acid evergreen duff and very cool soil temperatures that are nearly impossible to reproduce at lower elevations. Enjoy them in nature, and leave them alone!

CASTILLEJA RHEXIFOLIA

PLAINS PAINTBRUSH

Few plants dazzle travelers to the Rockies more than the variable paintbrushes that occur in nearly every ecosystem and elevation. One of the showiest grows throughout much of the Great Plains and at all elevations in the southernmost Rockies below tree line. The plains' paintbrush is a relative dwarf, usually well under a foot. Its large, petal-like bracts beneath the true flowers are often a luminous salmon-orange color that suggests flames on the prairie. It occurs in particular abundance throughout South Park and the San Luis Valley of central and southern Colorado, where acres of dry prairies bloom orange for weeks and months in summer.

SUBALPINE PAINTBRUSH

Most paintbrushes prefer hot, dry exposures among sagebrush and prairie grasses. But the subalpine paintbrush grows most abundantly in the wetter ranges of both the southern and northern Rockies, frequently near running water. The color of its bracts varies from deep scarlet and crimson (similar to the more common montane paintbrushes) to stunning magenta, fuchsia and art deco shades of mauve and pink. The subalpine species frequently grows alongside the cool yellow sulphur paintbrush (*Castilleja sulfurea*) and sometimes hybridizes with it, producing an astonishing range of intermediate shades.

CHRYSOTHAMNUS NAUSEOSUS

RABBITBRUSH

Western homeowners have a penchant for planting forsythias, despite the fact that they are severely frosted year after year when their buds are coaxed to bloom just in time for an Alberta clipper. At the other extreme is rabbitbrush, which routinely produces heaped mounds of golden bloom from August to early winter. Many species and innumerable forms of rabbitbrush occur in drier habitats at all elevations below tree line. The plant is intensely aromatic, forming billowy mounds of gray leaves that superficially resemble sagebrush near which it often grows.

Sagebrush is generally much more silvery than rabbitbrush and the flowers bloom even later in autumn--mostly in silver shades similar to the leaves. This plant looks lovely along endless stretches of straight highway, where it is often tangled with various lavender and violet asters. These, along with the crystal clear blue autumn skies, provide a perfect foil to the golden mounds of rabbitbrush.

Some nurseries sell rabbitbrush in selections--dwarf (a foot tall or less), intermediate, and tall (over 6 ft.). They can be lovely in city gardens, particularly when allowed to dry a bit.

CLAYTONIA MEGARHIZA

Alpine Spring Beauty

The rosette shape--where a plant produces a neat nosegay of succulent leaves in a circle around a taproot--appears often in nature, from rain forest epiphytes to hens and chicks or violets of the Andes. In the Colorado Rockies, the most famous rosette is that of alpine spring beauty, which produces a neat circle of overlapping, rubbery leaves 6" to 8" across. These vary from deep green to deep red at the end of the growing season. The spring beauty is a high alpine plant that seems to grow larger and more abundantly the higher one climbs. It is the most common and often most dominant ground cover on the tops of the highest peaks (over 13,000 ft.) from the southern Rockies northward into Canada.

Throughout the alpine summer, translucent 5-petalled white flowers veined in pink peek out from the leaves in a neat circle around the periphery of the rosette, making a picture of perfect symmetry and charm. Its nearest relatives include a number of willowy, early spring ephemerals with similar cup-shaped flowers, but with insubstantial foliage that dies down promptly after flowering to a deep-seated bulb. Alpine spring beauty belongs to the Purslane, or Portulaca family, most of which are succulents from hotter, drier regions. It's surprising, then, that the alpine species has conquered the highest peaks.

CLEMATIS COLUMBIANA

WESTERN CLEMATIS

Clematis is often associated with latticework and fences, where the varieties produce sumptuous displays of white or deep purple-blue in summer. Some species of clematis twine or climb in our native mountains, but others grow in more novel ways. Western clematis, for example, has slightly woody stems that grow at or below the soil level, making wide mats of ferny foliage in sparse woods throughout the Rockies.

The flowers consist of four large, lavender segments that do not flare widely. Their "nod" gives the whole plant a distinctive touch and slightly wind-blown look, like a crowd of kerchiefed maidens. This is especially common in Douglas fir forests at mid-elevations (8,000 to 10,000 ft.) on steep slopes. An alpine phase occurs on limestone in the middle Rockies, forming dense tufts of foliage with particularly luminous blue flowers-- one of our loveliest native plants.

Two vining clematis create a spectacle in late summer. The brassy yellow Oriental clematis with nodding flowers forms vast mats on barren roadsides throughout the Rockies. A small-flowered white clematis, "virgin's bower," is native to the lower foothills where it can festoon low trees, bushes and fencerows for miles.

CORYPHANTHA VIVIPARA

Purple Ball Cactus

Cactus may bring to mind hot deserts, but a number of native cacti prefer cool environments, living at tree line in some Intermountain ranges. The purple ball cactus is a variable species, common on the Great Plains and widespread in the Great Basin. It grows abundantly in southern high mountain valleys or on the dry steppe of Wyoming.

The ovoid body of this plant reaches 4" or more across. Each whorl of spines is produced at the tip of a swollen protuberance called a tubercle. Tubercles, along with the mid- to late-June bloom period, distinguish this cactus from the similar mountain ball with its more spherical shape and small tubercles. The latter usually finishes blooming by Memorial Day. Flowers of the mountain ball are pale pink, yellowish, or white; but the purple ball is a deep, glowing rose-purple, highlighted by the boss of bright yellow stamens in the middle. Ball cacti grow slowly in the wild and are subject to trampling by cattle.

Travelers are amazed at the abundance of jointed prickly pear cacti that climb the Rockies' hot southern slopes, nearly to timberline in drier ranges. A half dozen species of *Opuntia* are widespread in the lower mountains; even more occur to the south. On overgrazed range they can become a dominant ground cover. Even ranchers admire the huge waxy, multi-petalled flowers that usually open for just one day. Shades of yellow are common, though pink and carmine often dominate valleys. Dabble a finger among the hair-like stamens on a warm day and see them perform a magical dance.

CYPRIPEDIUM CALCEOLUS

Yellow Ladyslipper

Few plants have the allure of wild orchids, suggesting far-off places and exotic settings. And few plants excite wildflower lovers more than native lady slippers, which can grow in astonishing abundance in a few spots, yet be entirely absent over hundreds of miles of perfectly suitable habitat.

The yellow lady slipper grows over much of Eurasia and North America, but is becoming rarer south of the 50th parallel. In the Rockies it is known in only a few dozen locations, mostly on the easternmost ranges bordering the Great Plains, from 7000 to 10,000 ft.

Plants can grow up to 2 ft. tall. Flowers are usually 4" or more across, with straw-yellow corkscrew petals dangling from the giant yellow pouch. For a few weeks in June, this ladyslipper lights up the open aspen, pine, and fir forests, and startles flower lovers who happen onto a colony.

In Britain, this once abundant plant has been reduced to a single specimen, thanks to egotistical collectors. Because research shows that plants in the wild may be decades old, *never* pick and *never* dig any of these miraculous treasures.

DELPHINIUM NELSONII

NELSON'S LARKSPUR

Two principal kinds of larkspurs are common in the west. At higher elevations, in rich, moist woods and meadows, are tall delphiniums that somewhat resemble the garden giants, but with smaller flowers tending to a darker purple. Long before the tall delphiniums bloom, tiny larkspurs abound in dry pastures, especially among sagebrush throughout the west.

This group has many species, all of which emerge from swollen, bulb like roots. Like true bulbs, these larkspurs grow quickly in the spring, bloom, and then die down. Their flowers are an incredible deep blue, verging on indigo in some forms. In certain years they occur in such abundance that they resemble deep blue pools of color among the sage. Although these scenes delight wildflower lovers, they cause consternation among farmers, for members of the delphinium family are poisonous, and kill livestock every year.

Often they are confused with the equally poisonous monkshood--also in the buttercup family. All larkspurs have outstretched lobes and a modified petal forming a sack, or spur, that points upwards in back of the blossom. But the Columbia monkshood, the only species in the Rockies, has lobes that cup inward in a helmet-like shape, reminiscent of conquistadors. The flowers can be an inky, purple blue or strange greenish-white.

DODECATHEON PULCHELLUM

SHOOTING STAR

Often travelers are reminded of cyclamen when they first see shooting stars. This is not surprising since both belong to the Primrose family. Most species have five rose petals, strongly reflexed, like a dog pointing its head out a window. But the alpine shooting star *(Dodecatheon alpinum)* has only four petals.

Shooting stars usually grow where it's wet in spring--along pond margins, streams or in low, wet, meadows--but a few species grow in the drier prairie. They can occur in such abundance as to tinge a meadow red with their flowers (although a few species are white). Certain plants emit a very sweet, innocent perfume. The tips of their blossoms have fantastically intricate coloration--a tiny delicate stripe of red with bands of white and pink pencilling the nose of the bloom.

At lower elevations these streamlined primroses can reach 2 ft. in height with a dozen or more flowers. Often the same species gets shorter as the altitude increases, so alpine tundra plants are only 1"-2" high, sometimes with just a single flower. When purchasing a shooting star from a nursery or growing one from seed, do not be surprised when the whole plant disappears during the first hot days of summer. The genus is prone to summer dormancy, a wonderful strategy for evading drought, and comes back stronger the next spring.

DUGADIA HOOPESII

ORANGE SNEEZEWEED

By August of most years the Daisy family dominates vistas in the Rockies. In montane and subalpine woods, the largest and showiest composite is orange sneezeweed, a yard-tall daisy with 4" to 5" flower heads of a distinctive, burnt orange color. Unlike the smaller flowered helenium, to which this plant is allied, these flower heads take on a windswept, asymmetrical form that adds to their distinctiveness. Many travelers assume native plants are benign, but this one is poisonous to livestock, particularly sheep.

Orange sneezeweed can be distinguished from most other subalpine composites by its loose rosette of smooth, rubbery, strap-like leaves. Arnicas, for instance, usually have heart-shaped leaves with a dense coat of raspy hairs. They are particularly common in open conifer forests, forming vast colonies with their rhizomes-- underground stems. Their large flowers sometimes have droopy ray flowers as well, usually a soft yellow color.

The Rockies' most widespread and numerous late summer composites are the variable ragworts. The senecios can form giant clumps a yard or more high or even tiny ground covers. Their flowers never attain the large size of orange sneezeweed or even most arnicas, but our high mountain meadows would be quite different without these glorious yellow composites.

ECHINOCEREUS TRIGLOCHIDIATUS

CLARET CUP CACTUS

Most western cacti open their flowers in the morning and close them the evening of the same day. But one group of widespread clumping cacti, the claret cups, stay open for several days until they wither. This common name covers several species and many varieties of a small, hedgehog-like cactus which, over time, forms very large clumps. The waxy, scarlet flowers are shaped like badminton birdies. They usually start to bloom in May and last into early June.

Claret cup grows throughout the Colorado and Great Basin desert, among the sagebrush. It is particularly common on rocky outcrops of pinon-juniper woodlands, and is not uncommon as high as 8500 ft., where it grows on warm cliffs throughout the southern Rockies.

Fendler's hedgehog makes small clumps with 2 or 3 stems producing a 4" purple torch of bloom in June in pygmy forests of the southernmost Rockies. The only other abundant hedgehog cactus is the greenflowered hedgehog, with tiny stems only 2" or 3" high. It is virtually invisible in the short grasses of mountain parkland although it grows by the thousands from New Mexico to Montana. One usually finds it by the unfortunate act of stepping on the plant. If it's in full bloom, kneel down and smell the waxy, chartreuse, lime-scented flowers.

ERIOGONUM JAMESII v. XANTHUM

ALPINE BUCKWHEAT

Various buckwheats and sulphur flowers comprise one of the showiest groups of native plants. They occur at all altitudes and in nearly every soil and precipitation range except for dense woods and bogs. James alpine buckwheat lives above tree line in the southern Rockies of Colorado, but not universally. It prefers south facing slopes at or above timberline in the Mosquito, Sawatch and Front Ranges. Its leaves are 2" to 3" long and almost 1" across, forming tight mounds of glistening, silvery foliage. Plants are often a foot across, with flowering stems that practically rest on the cushion. The bright yellow flowers age quickly to burnt orange and deep red. This genus is a favorite of dried-flower enthusiasts and xeriscape gardeners, for the plants make an impact in a vase or in the garden.

In the high tundra of Idaho, Wyoming, and Montana, 5 or more species of tiny buckwheats can be found on warm, sunny slopes. Some, like the ovalleaf buckwheat, occur in bright shades from pure white, pink, and red, to deep orange and pert yellow. Others, like the caespitose buckwheat, are usually a bronzy red. They can form extensive mats, a foot or more across, and paint warm, dry slopes with color during the last months of the season. The plants are decorative even after seeds have been shed, since their round or oval leaves turn a deep purple in the colder months.

ERYTHRONIUM GRANDIFLORUM

GLACIER LILY

Lovers of eastern wildflowers are familiar with white or yellow trout lilies that occasionally can be found in deep woods blooming in early spring. Glacier or snow lilies are closely related, but their leaves lack the colorful spots found on the eastern species. Glacier lilies usually grow in untold thousands, thriving in a great variety of soils and exposures from dense spruce woods to high alpine tundra.

Each plant has a pair of broad, pointed green leaves that emerge on either side of the flower stem. The stem usually has a single flower, but exceptional specimens may have up to 7. The bright yellow flowers are exact miniatures of the turk's cap lilies that bloom in midsummer. They are pure yellow and exude a refreshing sweet fragrance.

Glacier lilies are particularly abundant in the northern Rockies, where they thrive among sagebrush meadows at mountain bases and climb to timberline on most of the peaks. They are quite common on the Going To Heaven Highway in Glacier N.P., more localized in the Tetons and Yellowstone N.P., and occur for a short distance just below tree line on the west side of Trail Ridge Road in Rocky Mt. N.P.

GENTIANA PARRYI

Parry's Gentian

Travelers to the Rockies are both excited and a little saddened to find the first cup gentians. They're excited because this is one of the bluest and showiest of native wildflowers. But by August when it comes into full bloom, the mornings often show hoarfrost on the ground, meaning winter is not far away.

Parry's gentian usually is found above 8000 ft., in rich meadows among dried grasses. Its stems are about a foot tall, ending in a cluster of 3 or more tubular, cup-shaped flowers. These are often white inside and deep blue outside the segments. A tuft of fringy hairs appears between each of the 5 petals, a characteristic of true gentians. A similar cup gentian occurs in the northern Rockies that has just a single flower on every stem. It prefers streamsides and boggy ground. Several species of narrowleaved gentians occur on the prairies of parklands and lower foothills. These have narrower clusters of flowers that do not open as wide.

Fringed gentians are abundant in Yellowstone and other high, cool parklands of the Rockies. These have only 4 petals, wildly slashed along their margins. Unlike most gentians, which form massive underground roots, this is an annual or perhaps biennial that must constantly regenerate from fresh seed--a good reason to resist picking it!

GERANIUM CAESPITOSUM

FREMONT'S GERANIUM

Several kinds of pink and purple flowered geraniums occur in the Rockies from Mexico to Canada. Fremont's geranium has flowers of a lighter pink than some species, with wonderful lines and pencillings on each petal. It is closely related to the hot red and pink pelargoniums (geraniums) that create fantastic spots of color in window boxes of mountain towns.

Geraniums native to the Rockies are very hardy plants. In addition to their splendid flowers, they have a second season of color in autumn when their leaves turn a deep orange and scarlet.

Richardsons geranium, common in middle altitude woodlands throughout the region, has pure white flowers in mid-summer. Sticky geranium superficially resembles Fremont's, but the leaves are covered with intensely aromatic sticky glands and the flowers are usually a dark rose-purple.

A close relative, filaree, has become one of the most widespread European weeds in the Rocky Mountains. It forms a neat rosette with lacy, gray foliage and an almost constant succession of small pink geranium flowers through the calendar year. It grows rather harmlessly along paths and roads and in overgrazed pasture. This is one of the few plants that blooms into midwinter.

LIFE ZONE CHART

Vaughn Reichelderfer

WHERE TO SEE WILDFLOWERS

During the summer months, travelers can find outstanding displays of wildflowers almost anywhere in the Rockies. This region contains a majority of America's National Parks and Forests where wildflower lovers can wander. Please respect fenced areas. Request permission to visit private property in writing or by phone in advance of arrival.

The complicated mountain terrain leads to dramatic juxtapositions of plants and life zones. Cactus and yuccas appear on hot slopes up to 10,000 ft. in the southern Rockies, with orchids and lilies blooming nearby in shady coves. Plants do not always grow where expected and they frequently venture far beyond altitudinal limits.

ARCTIC ALPINE - Above 9,500 ft. in north, 12,000 ft. in southern Rockies. Common trees: dwarf bristlecone and limber pine. Wildflowers: alpine clover, alpine spring beauty, moss campion, old man of the mountain, Hall's penstemon, sky pilot, fairy primrose, alpine buckwheat, alpine cushion phlox

SUBALPINE OR HUDSONIAN - Above 8,500 ft. in north, 10,000 in south. Common trees: subalpine fir and Engelmann spruce. Wildflowers: globeflower, mule's ears, twinflower, orange sneezeweed, glacier lily, subalpine paintbrush, fairyslipper, marsh marigold, Parry's gentian, narcissus flowered anemone, Whipple's penstemon, little red elephant, purple monkey flower, yellow monkey flower, Parry's primrose

MONTANE - Above 6,000 ft. in north, 8,000 in south. Common trees: aspen, Douglas fir, lodgepole pine. Wildflowers: mariposa lily, golden banner, western clematis, blue flax, wood lily, shooting star, Fremont's geranium, Colorado columbine, Nelson's larkspur, yellow ladyslipper, fairy trumpet

FOOTHILLS - Above 4,000 ft. in north, 6,000 ft. in south. Common trees: ponderosa pine, western red cedar, Douglas fir. Wildflowers: pasqueflower, creeping hollyberry, bitter root, bracted alumroot, prickly poppy, rosy ball cactus, claret cup cactus.

PLAINS AND PLATEAUX - Below 4,000 ft. in north, 6,000 ft. in south. Common trees: plains' cottonwood, scrub oak, New Mexican locust. Wildflowers: cowboy's delight, plains' paintbrush, rabbitbrush, languid ladies, perky sue, narrowleaf penstemon, Nuttall's violet, Nuttall's evening primrose

There are active Native Plant Societies in every Rocky Mountain state that can be contacted through a local botanic garden. Many have intensive field trips led by experts. Nurseries and garden centers also offer a wide range of native perennials, wildflowers, and shrubs for landscaping. Among the major botanic gardens in the Rocky Mt. region:

Denver Botanic Gardens, 1000 York St., Denver, Colorado 80206. This 24-acre site contains many gardens that feature native plants as well as those from similar climates around the world. There is a superb botanical library and a knowledgeable staff with volunteers, 24 hour information line: (303)331-4000.

Betty Ford Alpine Garden, adjacent to Gerald Ford Park and Amphitheatre in Vail Village, Colorado, has outstanding display gardens featuring native and showy exotic plants in a natural setting.

HEUCHERA BRACTEATA

ALUMROOT

The patient traveler in the Rockies eventually will find a few plants of some species of alumroot. Nearly a dozen species occur in the region, most of which grow best in the tiny crevices of cliffs. Their leaves are the size of a coin--from dime to 50-cent piece--depending on how much moisture or shade they obtain. The leaf margins can be toothed or quite smooth, depending on the species, and the flowering stems likewise can vary from a few to nearly 24" tall.

Most alumroots have small but attractive bell-shaped flowers in white or even pink. Bracted alumroot flowers are a strange chartreuse color that distinguishes them at a distance. They bloom in June and July, lighting up dark granitic crevices with their lunar glow. This species is most common in the central ranges of the Rockies of Colorado and Wyoming.

Travelers up Pikes Peak might see Hall's alumroot, a particularly attractive white-flowered plant that suggests lily of the valley. On Sandia Peak near Albuquerque look for the showy pink-flowered, endemic to that mountain. The pale rose species *(Heuchera rubescens)* is abundant throughout the Pacific drainage of the Rockies. Best-known of all alumroot is the bright red coral bells that thrives in gardens worldwide and occurs as a wildflower in the mountains of New Mexico and Arizona, at the very southern tip of the Rockies.

Old Man of the Mountain   HYMENOXYS GRANDIFLORA

OLD MAN OF THE MOUNTAIN

Few travelers will have trouble identifying the Old Man of the Mountain, for this is the largest flowering alpine plant in the Rockies. Imagine a sunflower buried up to its neck and you have this distinctive native plant. One of the most impressive sights in the tundra is a host of old men sunflowers looking east on a sunny day. Some say the flowers turn with the sun, but they do seem to have a decided preference for the east. This is one of the few alpine plants that dies once it blooms. The colonies of hairy, cutleaf tufts of young plants may take 5 or more years to reach blooming stage.

These astonishing flowers can reach 5" or more in width. As with other composites, each flower head actually consists of dozens of individual florets--a sort of giant bouquet on each stem. Individual plants can produce three or more flowers per stem, but secondary flowers are usually much smaller. The Old Man frequents sunny pastures above tree line, from northern New Mexico to Montana and Idaho.

PERKY SUE

An English botanist once suggested that the Rockies be renamed the Daisy Chain, because of the abundance of daisies here. Perky Sue is common but variable over much of the region. The lowland form that grows in foothills and on the prairies has low tufts of gray-green leaves. Its yellow daisies on short stalks can reach a foot high in very favorable seasons. On tundra, the leaves are shorter, covered in long silky hair, and the flowers are nearly stemless.

IPOMOPSIS AGGREGATA

Fairy Trumpets

A number of tall, wand-like plants with scarlet trumpets can be found throughout the Rockies. One of the most common is the fairy trumpet, a biennial in the phlox family that has spidery, five petalled flowers of bright coral red, pink, or often pure white.

The first year this plant germinates from seed it produces a frosty, filigreed rosette, as complicated and decorative as a doily. The second year it skyrockets higher and higher--often more than a yard--producing a shower of 3" to 5" trumpets of coralline color.

They bloom nearly all season. Fairy trumpets represent a number of distinctive races and even species of Gilia or Ipomopsis. These occur throughout the sagebrush middle elevations of the Rockies, growing through pinon-juniper woodlands, montane and subalpine levels (usually on sunnier, drier slopes), and even approaching the alpine level along roadsides and in warmer areas. Some kind of fairy trumpet can be found in any state west of the Mississippi. They are favorite plants of hummingbirds and travelers, both of whom can often be seen hovering nearby.

LEWISIA REDIVIVA

BITTER ROOT

At first sight the bitter root looks much like a water lily growing on solid land. Gravelly slopes and sagebrush meadows can sport countless thousands of this ethereal flower in the softest shades of pink. Each plant can produce many individual blossoms in late spring and early summer, although three to five is perhaps typical. Each flower is usually wider than 3", with a dozen or more individual petals. The tuft of narrow leaves often withers by bloom time, only to emerge again toward the end of the following winter.

The bark around the root is apparently responsible for the bitterness, but native Indians nevertheless used these plants as an important source of nutrients. They have been gathered in tremendous numbers by various tribes of the northern Rockies, although the quantity of bitter root today seems as common as ever.

These plants prefer gravelly open areas among sagebrush, from 3000 ft. in the northern part of their range to well over 9000 toward the south. Most other native species of *Lewisia* in the Rockies are much smaller and less showy.

LILIUM PHILADELPHICUM

Wood Lily

As the summer solstice approaches, lucky hikers occasionally stumble upon colonies of wood lilies. They are easily recognizable, being probably the largest flowered native plant in the Rockies. Their waxy, scarlet flowers measure nearly 6" across. Wood lilies are most common in Aspen groves along rivers. In montane elevations, they often grow out of juniper bushes, particularly in the front ranges of the Rockies. But near roads or where farmers have grazed their cattle heavily, these flowers are rare, for cows love to eat the big, succulent flowers and city folk can't resist digging them.

It is possible to grow wood lilies from seed, but travelers are encouraged never to touch wild colonies of them. It is said that even a tiny touch of salt from the fingers or a person's lingering scent is enough to attract deer and elk. These animals invariably decapitate the flowers carrying the human scent.

Wood lilies occur sparingly in northern New Mexico, even in the San Juan Mountains of southwestern Colorado, but they are much more common in the northern Rockies, and grow quite far onto the grasslands as well.

LINNAEA BOREALIS

TWINFLOWER

From late June through August, dark subalpine forests throughout the Rockies are often graced with the tiny, twin bells of this most delicate of honeysuckle vines. These are worth examining closely, for the inside of each pink or appleblossom white bell is often filled with hairs and much darker rose red pencilling. Even a tiny sprig exudes a rich, distinctive confectionary fragrance. Fortunate travelers can walk into a grove with thousands of flowers, where the ethereal, sweet scent can be exhilarating.

There is a gothic feeling to subalpine fir and spruce woodlands. Twinflower is only one of a number of delicate wildlings including pyrolas, moneses, pipsissewas, cornel and a host of tiny orchids, lilies and primulas. These charming plants can turn a dark woodland into a fairyland of miniature jewel-like wildflowers.

Botanists have an added reason to revere twinflower: Carolus Linnaeus' student, Gronovius, named the plant for this father of modern botany when he noticed that the great botanist somehow had overlooked a plant that grew abundantly right around his cottage. Linnaeus is always depicted holding a twig of twinflower in his portraits, a plant he loved because, like himself, it was "so modest."

LINUM LEWISII

Blue Flax

Although there are blue flax in many parts of the northern hemisphere, the Rocky Mountain varieties capture the imaginations of all wildflower lovers. In lower elevations, nearly every meadow has a smattering of foot-tall stems with satiny, five-petalled flowers in a particularly soft blue color. Higher up the mountain, and in the northern Rockies, the flowers are often a piercing sapphire. Plants can vary from a few inches tall on alpine tundra in the Bighorn Mountains, to robust, 2-ft. giants in rich meadows.

The flowers are freshest in the early morning. Later in the day, a large plant can have quite an undercarpet of blue after the petals have fallen. This is a plant that knows how to prepare for the daily ritual of late day summer thundershowers in the Rocky Mountains.

Cultivated flax has established occasionally in the foothills of the Rockies, mostly as an escapee from agricultural experiments. It superficially resembles the native species, but is annual and more finely textured. Perennial garden flax, a native of Europe, is slightly stockier and always a deep blue. It is frequently grown in gardens and has been used in occasional roadside wildflower mixes.

MAHONIA REPENS

CREEPING HOLLYBERRY

Few plants provide a longer season of color and interest in the Rockies than the creeping hollyberry. Sometime as early as April, travelers can find the rich clusters of 5-petalled flowers spreading a rich fragrance through dry woods and rocky hillsides, from the plains well into the montane elevations.

In summer the bright blue-purple fruit provides a wonderful foil for the fresh, glossy evergreen leaves. These often take on a deep purple tone in winter, some leaflets even turning scarlet, which is particularly lovely against the fresh yellow blooms in early spring.

The plant grows thick enough in places that it's possible to gather sufficient fruit to make a tart, sweet jam. Most of us are content to enjoy the plant's year-around antics. Today, local nurseries are growing increasing quantities of these young plants, and it makes a striking, drought-tolerant native to have at home.

The native barberries have one more useful feature: their roots and stems contain a bright orange alkaloid called berberine which has a wide spectrum of herbal and medicinal uses. It has been used to reduce fevers, as a mild laxative, and as an antibacterial wash. Still, this four-season shrub's primary attraction is its glossy, holly-like leaves that are never lovelier than in the winter, when they look just like holly in the snow.

MERTENSIA LANCEOLATA

Languid Ladies

The Rocky Mountain region is the center of diversity for the genus *Mertensia*. Travelers can find tiny species just a few inches tall growing near giant streamside plants 4 ft. or taller. Few plants are as widespread or beloved as the narrow-leaved languid lady. It can be found in countless thousands on the high plains near the Rockies, in open parkland among ponderosa pine of the foothills, or growing with sagebrush in the high mountain parklands.

Everywhere the languid lady grows, it forms a graceful, vase-like cluster of stems with narrow leaves 1" to 2" long. These are covered with a powdery blue bloom of wax that gives the plant a ghostly look. This feature probably helps protect it from the fierce sun and long periods of drought that occur over much of its range. The cluster of inch-long pinky blue bells are produced in small clusters from the upper leaf axils. They can chime quietly from May to June, depending on altitude.

At higher altitudes, on wet subalpine slopes, another *Mertensia* occurs. Its streamside chiming bells can grow well over a meter in areas of high rainfall, producing an endless succession of little bells from the leaf axils. As a result, it blooms throughout the summer season. Typically the flowers are bright pink in bud, turning a powdery baby blue as the flower ages.

MIMULUS GUTTATUS

YELLOW MONKEY FLOWER

Late summer means daisies all across America. But in the Rockies, wet streamsides and bogs often fill with a host of monkey flowers as well. The most common of these is one of the showiest. From a tiny tuft of soft green leaves emerges a remarkable succession of snapdragon-like yellow monkey faces that grin along streams during July and August and into the autumn. Common yellow monkey flowers reach heights of 3" to 5" or more. Roots can stay submerged much of the season, but seem to grow particularly well in mounds of verdant moss next to water.

PURPLE MONKEY FLOWER

Sometimes found next to the tiny yellow variety is the giant purple monkey flower. It grows not only a foot or more high, but has flowers up to 2" long and well over an inch wide. Lewis and Clark first found the purple monkey flower in the northern Rockies, where it still grows in tremendous profusion in late summer. It is most abundant along tiny rivulets just below tree line, although it does grow above timberline as well. This monkey flower extends from British Columbia and Alberta, southward to Wyoming and a short way into northwestern Colorado.

OENOTHERA NUTTALLII

NUTTALL'S EVENING PRIMROSE

At a distance it's possible to mistake evening primrose blossoms for flourescent white paper; some have such luminous whiteness as to shame a piece of spotless stationery. These huge white, pink, or occasionally yellow flowers have a crepe-like texture. A patient observer can watch them pop open in the cool of evening; by next morning, some forms will age to a luminous pink or tangerine. On cloudy or very cool days, the flowers may stay fresh and white.

The stemless Nuttall's evening primrose seems to prefer gravelly roadcut environments. Quite tall and robust, it thrives on sandy pastures bordering the Great Plains. This lovely plant was named for Thomas Nuttall, the first botanist to traverse and collect extensively in the Rocky Mountains.

Many species of fragrant yellow evening primroses also occur in the foothills of the Rockies. Some, like the lavender leaved evening primrose, make small shrubs a foot or more across that belie their common name and bloom during the daylight hours. A few, like Hooker's evening primrose, are biennial, producing a neat rosette the first year, but in the second year sending up a 3-ft. or higher stalk with countless tiny yellow flowers that open each evening for most of the summer.

PEDICULARIS GROENDLANDICA

LITTLE RED ELEPHANT

Certain flowers seem to have been designed specifically to capture the imaginations of children. Among these are tiny red elephants. As summer peaks, the wet meadows at higher elevations from New Mexico to Canada often turn a deep purple-pink with innumerable clusters of red elephant flowers. Each stem may have a hundred or more miniature trophy heads less than an inch long.

The genus *Pedicularis*, to which red elephants belong, is well represented in the western U.S. Its real center of diversity lies in the Himalayas and western China, where dozens of species occur in every hue of the rainbow. Originating in such rainy mountains, the plants have developed convoluted animal-like shapes to protect the pollen and pistils from constant rain and mist. Tradition has saddled plants in this genus with the unhappy name of lousewort--presumably because of an imagined resemblence to lice, or perhaps because they are a remedy for louse bites?

As with paintbrush, louseworts apparently practice a subtle parasitism on the roots of neighboring plants. They are in such delicate equilibrium with their hosts that transplanted sods quickly perish; few have grown a lousewort successfully from seed to bloom.

PENSTEMON WHIPPLEANUS

PENSTEMONS

Claude Barr, pioneer horticulturist of the Great Plains, considered the narrowleaf to be the loveliest of the many native penstemons. Beard tongues, as narrowleafs are sometimes called, grow at all elevations and in a bewildering variety of microclimates throughout the Rockies. They can be found on warm, dry prairies and rocky hillsides up to 7000 ft. in the foothills of the southern and middle Rockies, in the Uinta Basin, Canyonlands, and through much of New Mexico.

The narrow, shining leaves are coated with blue wax--quite different from other native penstemons. In most soils the inch-wide flowers are an unmistakable robin's egg blue, although this can vary to pink or even purple shades in acidic soils. Plants are usually a foot or slightly taller, although a dwarf race occurs on the Laramie Plains that barely exceeds 6". Gardeners growing this or other penstemons should give them a very gravelly soil and try to keep from watering them too much. They will grow much better and live longer if they are not pampered.

Many miles of roadcuts are painted bright blue in summer by Hall's penstemon. Only a few species live in the alpine tundra, and this is perhaps the showiest of them. It produces a low tuft or mat of grassy, narrow leaves a few inches long that turn deep purple in the colder months. In July and August the tuft is usually obscured below a forest of 4" to 6" stems with many flowers each. The 1-1/2" blossoms are a deep violet-blue. Hall's is restricted to the higher peaks of Colorado and is particularly common in the Saguache and Mosquito ranges, and in Elk Park on Pike's Peak.

PHLOX CONDENSATA

Probably the most widespread penstemon at higher altitudes in the west is Whipple's, the most common species in subalpine woodlands. It forms a mat of oval leaves that generally produce 5 to 10 stems from a foot to well over 2 ft. tall. Flower color is extremely variable, from deep blue-purple in Utah and Arizona to claret and wine-purple in New Mexico and southwestern Colorado. The more northerly races are often a strange violet-black rarely seen in flowers. Near albino colonies that vary from lemonade to bright yellow are common on many mountains. Whipple's is easily recognizable by a characteristic nodding pose. Its flowers have a decided pout and frequently somber coloration--a penstemon that could use an anti-depressant!

ALPINE CUSHION PHLOX

Few plants impress European visitors more than our native phloxes that are as common on American mountains as phlox are in European gardens. Like penstemons, paintbrush and shooting stars, phloxes are true red-white-and-blue Americans, with only one species in each of these large genera crossing over to Eurasia. In the Rockies, phlox are abundant among sagebrush pastures, in high mountain meadows, even in lodgepole pine woodlands. The high alpine phloxes form rock hard cushions that are completely hidden with dime-sized flowers for much of the growing season. These 5-petalled, starlike blossoms are incredibly fragrant--definitely stop to smell these flowers!

POLEMONIUM VISCOSUM

SKY PILOT

One alpine flower that every novice learns quickly is the sky pilot. These lovely ball-like clusters of sapphire blue flowers with bright yellow-orange anthers have a sweet fragrance. Step on the fern-like leaves, however, and a skunky smell will follow you for miles! Unkind hikers call this skunkweed, but pocket-gopherweed would be more appropriate, for this striking native alpine plant is nearly restricted to pocket gopher diggings within its range. It spreads to yard-wide colonies wherever the soil has been recently disturbed, and blooms best where gophers are most active. Thanks to the little rodents, there's plenty of oxygen and fertilizer in their freshly tilled furrows--a perfect example of symbiosis between plant and animal world.

A number of *Polemoniums* species occur at lower levels in the Rockies. Most have leaves cut into a series of ladder-like leaflets--hence the common name Jacob's ladder. Some form low ground covers in deep spruce-fir forests; others make husky clumps, up to a meter high, in rich meadows. Brandegee's Jacob's ladder resembles straw yellow sky pilot and sometimes is found growing with it, especially along the east end of Trail Ridge in Rocky Mt. N.P. It grows sporadically at lower altitudes, from southern New Mexico to Wyoming, usually in the crevices of granite cliffs.

PRIMULA ANGUSTIFOLIA

PRIMROSES

Primroses are associated with high mountains throughout the northern hemisphere. A half dozen species of *Primula* occur in the Rockies, but the only one spread abundantly over wide areas of tundra is the tiny fairy primrose in the south. This is one of the first flowers to bloom as the snow melts, so mid-summer travelers see only the last few bedraggled blossoms. Above 12,000 ft. in mid-June, however, whole mountainsides can be tinted pink with thousands of this miniature native wildflower.

Most plants consist of only a few crowns, each with 3 or 4 narrow leaves a few inches long, and only 1 or 2 flowers rising from each crown. Occasional robust plants with 2 or 3 flowers per stem occur in moister, richer habitats. *Primula cusickiana*, Cusick's primrose, grows very similarly in Idaho, but with flowers of a rich blue-violet.

Unlike its smaller cousin, Parry's primrose can grow 2 ft. tall or more in rich soils. This is the common streamside primrose throughout the Rocky Mountains. It is most abundant along alpine freshets, at and below tree line, and rarely grows below 11,000 ft. in its southerly stations. The flower clusters can have a dozen or more individual blooms, 1-1/2" across and of a deep rose-magenta color. Their pungent smell reminds many people of musk, and can be quite offensive, but to most wildflower lovers, it is the queen of American *primulas*.

PULSATILLA PATENS

PASQUEFLOWER

Few plants grow over a wider altitudinal range than the western pasqueflower. It dots the Great Plains prairie of South Dakota, where it is the state flower, and is also common in open ponderosa parklands in the foothills of the Rockies, carpeting the forest floor and meadows. Each clump consists of coarsely cut, quite hairy leaves, and the opalescent lavender-blue flower cup. These clumps are roughly the size and shape of a hen's egg, on a stem 3"-5" tall.

The pasqueflower occurs sporadically through Aspen groves up to subalpine meadows, venturing onto warm slopes in the tundra where it waits to bloom until July or even August--months after it has finished blooming far below on the plains. As the flower fades, it forms a very striking mop-like seed head.

Much confusion has occasioned the naming of this plant, since botanists waver whether to lump all pasqueflowers into the giant genus *Anemone* or keep them as a segregate. Westerners have added to the confusion by referring to the plant as prairie crocus. True crocus grow only in Eurasia and are monocots belonging to the Iris family. Its common name, pasqueflower, alludes to the paschal, or Easter season when pulsatillas are usually in bloom. The roots have been used since Roman times to produce a bright green dye for Easter eggs--perhaps another explanation for the name.

SILENE ACAULIS

MOSS CAMPION

Most of our best-known Rocky Mountain plants, like beardtongues and buckwheats, are restricted to this region, but some can be found on mountains all over the world. Moss campion is as abundant on the bluffs of Alaska and the high ridges of the Alps as it is in the Rockies. When not in bloom, the foliage resembles a tuft of moss, sometimes a foot or more across. The 5-petalled flowers remind some people of dianthus and others of phlox, although the blunt, square end of each petal is unlike any phlox, and there are no native *Dianthi* in North America south of Alaska. Albino flowers are common in some areas; in others, the pinkness of the flowers is surprisingly variable. Look for moss campion on exposed ridges well above tree line, occasionally growing in sparse grass. Sometimes it appears in places that have running water in the early season when the snowmelt peaks.

A great variety of campions grow here. Most have white flowers and swollen, bag-like calyces that give the plants a whimsical appearance. The laciniate campion lives at moderate elevations in New Mexico along the southern fringe of the Rockies. It has sticky gray foliage and a constant succession of ragged, orange stars that bloom from late spring to frost. Peterson's campion is a very local species that forms thin mats on the steep limestone screes of central Utah. Here the stars are a rosy pink, and the flowers nod in a shy fashion.

SPHAERALCEA COCCINEA

Cowboy's Delight

Orange is not a common color among flowers, and the pale tangerine of cowboy's delight is particularly unusual. This is one of the very few mallows that occur in dry pastures in the Rockies. It forms thin mats that spread from rhizomes, ranging from a foot to a yard across. Each blossom is about an inch across, but several flowers are produced on each stem. More and more flowers emerge if summer rains are heavy. On overgrazed pasture, cowboy's delight can form a dominant ground cover. In late June and July, acres of the west are tinted a soft orange when it is in full bloom.

Along the western base of the Rockies, a number of taller *sphaeralceas* occur, many of which reach one meter in good years. The flower color of these western mallows varies from deep rose-purple to the more common bright yellows.

Another striking mallow found locally on the Great Plains is winecups. Here the foliage is quite deeply divided in bird's foot fashion, and is a deep blue-green color. The mat produces an endless succession of hot pink, cup-shaped blossoms that appear in a heavy flush in late spring, and more or less thickly through summer, depending on rainfall. It seems to do best on sandy or gravelly prairie soils.

THERMOPSIS RHOMBIFOLIA

Golden Banner

Yellow pea flowers are rare in the west. The only common yellow peas are various species of golden banner, abundant in open woods and meadows from 6000 to 10,000 ft. Dwarf golden banner *(T. divaricarpa)* is particularly common in open groves of ponderosa pine in the lower foothills. Mountain golden banner grows up to a yard, preferring rich, moist aspen forests on Colorado's Western Slope.

T. rhombifolia is most common in the lower foothills and Great Plains, often growing in barren shale and sparse grasses. Many travelers assume this is a yellow flowcred lupine, but native Rocky Mountain lupines tend to lavender, pink, and white. Lupine leaves are radially symmetrical, arranged in a cartwheel fashion, while golden banner produces its leaves in a ladder-like arrangement. Again, the genus is primarily concentrated in western North America, although there is a strong second center of diversity in China and the Himalayas.

TRIFOLIUM NANUM

ALPINE CLOVER

A half dozen species of clover abound on tundra of the Rockies. Most produce large, round heads of deep rose-pink or pale apricot. On gravelly ridges at the highest elevations, dwarf alpine clover forms tight mats of reduced foliage. Rather than bunching its florets into a ball-like head, so common among clovers, the alpine species has virtually stemless blossoms with only 1 or 2 florets on each attenuated stalk.

Flower hunters will notice the sweet, honey-like fragrance of meadow clover, and may mistake it for a cushion milk-vetch, since there are hundreds of native milk-vetches at lower elevations in the west. But the only alpine milk-vetches above tree line are lax in growth, or have more gray leaves and a somewhat prickly texture in leaf and bloom. When in doubt, bend down and sniff it. Most alpine cushion plants produce strong fragrances to lure the relatively sparse insect fauna that live at high elevations. Alpine clover, however, emits the same sweet fragrance as low altitude meadow clovers.

While alpine clover produces just 1 or 2 florets along the flowering nodes, Parry's clover errs in the opposite direction. Here, dozens of florets are packed into a giant head the size of a golf ball. Its color is a rich purple-pink, and it often forms dense tufts along alpine and subalpine freshets. It's not impossible to find Parry's and alpine clover growing together--proof that genetics, not environment, shape these species.

VIOLA NUTTALLII

NUTTALL'S VIOLET

Is there a greater oxymoron than a yellow violet? The long narrow leaves don't remind most travelers of violets, but the rather large blossoms are distinctly violet-shaped. Nuttall's violet can be very common in spring on warm slopes throughout the Great Plains and lower foothills. Two months later they pop up again just below tree line in a number of mountain ranges on the east face of the Rockies. The common yellow violet with much rounder leaves on the Pacific drainage of the Rockies is *Viola purpurea*--a double oxymoron!

There are also lavender, blue, and even white violets in the Rockies. Perhaps our most common species is also the smallest, a microform of the widespread western meadow violet *(viola adunca)*, with leaves not much bigger than a capital "O". It has not seen fit to persist in cultivation in the Rockies. The only Rocky Mountain violet that does manage to grow quite lushly in the garden is the Canada violet. This is rather local in montane and subalpine woods, where it can rise to a foot in height. Its innocent white or pale lavender violets grow thickly over a long season. The plant often branches repeatedly to form a round, almost bushy mound. Unlike most western violets, it grows well in gardens.

WYETHIA AMPLEXICAULIS

Mule's Ears

Mule's ears, and its close cousin balsam root, are largely plants of the western slopes of the Rocky Mountains, where rivers drain the Pacific or into the Great Basin. Although the western slopes are often very wet, they receive the bulk of their moisture as snow, with heavy downpours in early spring. By mid-summer, the meadows where these giant daisies grow are often burned, and these husky plants completely disappear.

The eastern face of the Rockies receives less precipitation, but a greater proportion falls as summer thundershowers. By mid-summer in the east, travelers can see an incredible array of daisies in full bloom.

On the plains bordering the Rockies, in Wyoming and Montana, the purple coneflower dominates the landscape with its giant purple cartwheels. Black-eyed Susans in many species occur at lower elevations from June to frost. Along roadsides, in many valleys and plateaux, the most abundant Composite is the wild form of the domestic sunflower, which brings the season to an end in late September or October. It forms giant fountains of brassy bloom up to 8 ft. high in most swales throughout the Great Plains, particularly in the high valleys of the southernmost Rockies. This is a final sunburst that puts the year to bed, until the eastern daisies start to bloom again in late winter. No wonder the Englishman thought the Rockies should be called "the Daisy Chain"!